Small Talk

Eight Short Plays by
Eric Fallen

A Samuel French Acting Edition

New York Hollywood London Toronto

SAMUELFRENCH.COM

Copyright © 2011 by Eric Fallen
ALL RIGHTS RESERVED

CAUTION: Professionals and amateurs are hereby warned that *SMALL TALK* is subject to a Licensing Fee. It is fully protected under the copyright laws of the United States of America, the British Commonwealth, including Canada, and all other countries of the Copyright Union. All rights, including professional, amateur, motion picture, recitation, lecturing, public reading, radio broadcasting, television and the rights of translation into foreign languages are strictly reserved. In its present form the play is dedicated to the reading public only.

The amateur and professional live stage performance rights to *SMALL TALK* are controlled exclusively by Samuel French, Inc., and licensing arrangements and performance licenses must be secured well in advance of presentation. PLEASE NOTE that amateur Licensing Fees are set upon application in accordance with your producing circumstances. When applying for a licensing quotation and a performance license please give us the number of performances intended, dates of production, your seating capacity and admission fee. Licensing Fees are payable one week before the opening performance of the play to Samuel French, Inc., at 45 W. 25th Street, New York, NY 10010.

Licensing Fee of the required amount must be paid whether the play is presented for charity or gain and whether or not admission is charged.

Professional/Stock licensing fees quoted upon application to Samuel French, Inc.

For all other rights than those stipulated above, apply to: Samuel French, Inc. 45 West 25th Street, New york, NY 10010.

Particular emphasis is laid on the question of amateur or professional readings, permission and terms for which must be secured in writing from Samuel French, Inc.

Copying from this book in whole or in part is strictly forbidden by law, and the right of performance is not transferable.

Whenever the play is produced the following notice must appear on all programs, printing and advertising for the play: "Produced by special arrangement with Samuel French, Inc."

Due authorship credit must be given on all programs, printing and advertising for the play.

ISBN 978-0-573-60120-0 Printed in U.S.A. #29791

No one shall commit or authorize any act or omission by which the copyright of, or the right to copyright, this play may be impaired.

No one shall make any changes in this play for the purpose of production.

Publication of this play does not imply availability for performance. Both amateurs and professionals considering a production are strongly advised in their own interests to apply to Samuel French, Inc., for written permission before starting rehearsals, advertising, or booking a theatre.

No part of this book may be reproduced, stored in a retrieval system, or transmitted in any form, by any means, now known or yet to be invented, including mechanical, electronic, photocopying, recording, videotaping, or otherwise, without the prior written permission of the publisher.

MUSIC USE NOTE

Licensees are solely responsible for obtaining formal written permission from copyright owners to use copyrighted music in the performance of this play and are strongly cautioned to do so. If no such permission is obtained by the licensee, then the licensee must use only original music that the licensee owns and controls. Licensees are solely responsible and liable for all music clearances and shall indemnify the copyright owners of the play and their licensing agent, Samuel French, Inc., against any costs, expenses, losses and liabilities arising from the use of music by licensees.

IMPORTANT BILLING AND CREDIT REQUIREMENTS

All producers of *SMALL TALK* must give credit to the Author of the Play in all programs distributed in connection with performances of the Play, and in all instances in which the title of the Play appears for the purposes of advertising, publicizing or otherwise exploiting the Play and/or a production. The name of the Author *must* appear on a separate line on which no other name appears, immediately following the title and *must* appear in size of type not less than fifty percent of the size of the title type.

CONTENTS

Perfect Weather 7
The Merry-Go-Round 17
Communion 25
The Monster 33
Basic Plumbing. 43
The Driving Range. 51
Behind the Wheel. 59
The Inclusion 69

PERFECT WEATHER

CAST OF CHARACTERS

PAUL: In his forties.
JIM: In his thirties.

PERFECT WEATHER was first presented at the 35th Samuel French Off-Off Broadway Short Play Festival at the Lions Theatre on July 16th, 2010. The performance was produced and directed by Eric Michael Gillett. The Production Stage Manager was Russ Weatherford. The cast was as follows:

PAUL .... Richard O'Brien
JIM .... Nathan Spiteri

(*AT RISE: Early morning on a sidewalk along Central Park.* JIM *sits on a bench at centerstage. He wears camouflage cargo shorts and a T-shirt. There is a large backpack on the ground between his feet. He removes a breakfast sandwich from a paper bag. He peels away some foil and takes a bite.* PAUL *enters from stage right. He's wearing a simple dark suit and aviator sunglasses. He takes a seat next to* JIM. *He leans back and stares up into the trees.*)

PAUL. This weather is perfect.

(JIM *does not respond. He takes a coffee out of the paper bag, opens and sips.*)

What do you think? Am I right?

JIM. It's nice.

PAUL. I just love it.

JIM. It is nice.

PAUL. I mean, some people enjoy the heat. *(pause)* Not me. I can't function when it gets too hot.

JIM. Yeah.

PAUL. Some people can just deal with it. The heat. It's in their blood. *(long pause)* What about you?

JIM. Me?

PAUL. Yeah. Can you function in the heat? I can't function in the heat.

JIM. I prefer this weather.

PAUL. Yeah. This weather really is perfect.

(PAUL *takes out his Blackberry and types a message. He puts it away.*)

So what ya got there, an egg and cheese?

JIM. Uhm, it's an egg, cheese and sausage.

PAUL. Nice. I love the breakfast sandwich. Beats the hell out of a bowl of dry flakes, right?

JIM. Yeah.

PAUL. I used to eat those things like they were going out of style. Just egg and cheese…with ketchup, salt and pepper. *(pause)* But, no more. *(pause)* I was on the Atkins. Ever try that? The Atkins diet?

JIM. No.

PAUL. No. Well, you're a pretty skinny guy. Naturally skinny, right? *(pause)* I've been battling the bulge since I was a kid. It's in the genes.

(There's a long silence. **PAUL** *takes out his Blackberry again and sends another message.)*

So, I'm Paul, by the way.

JIM. Jim.

PAUL. Nice to meet you. *(pause)* So hey, what's that accent you got there?

JIM. Accent?

PAUL. Yeah. I detect an accent.

JIM. I didn't know I had an accent.

PAUL. Really? I thought I picked up on something there. Just faintly.

JIM. No. I mean, Long Island…

PAUL. No. Never mind. It must just be my ear. I thought I picked up a foreign accent.

JIM. No. That's funny. No one's ever said that before.

PAUL. It's my ear.

(Long pause.)

So, I don't mean to be nosey, but what do you do, Jim?

JIM. What do I do?

PAUL. Yeah. I mean, it's eight o'clock in the morning, you've got your egg and cheese on a roll…and your big backpack there. *(pause)* Do you work in the neighborhood?

JIM. I'm kind of between jobs right now.

PAUL. Oh yeah?

JIM. I mean, I do have a job, but it's just…you know…

PAUL. It's temporary.

JIM. Right.

PAUL. A stepping stone…to the real job.

JIM. Exactly.

PAUL. So, where is it? This temporary job?

JIM. I work at Starbucks.

PAUL. Oh. Very cool. I like the Americano. The Americano is my drink. Do you like the Americano?

JIM. Yes. I actually do. I like the iced Americano.

PAUL. Oh yes. Yes. The iced Americano…very yummy.

JIM. Yes.

PAUL. So good.

JIM. So good.

PAUL. The flavor.

JIM. Strong.

PAUL. Yes. Just perfect. A perfect drink. *(pause)* So you're a "Barista."

JIM. Well…

PAUL. I mean, for now, you're a Barista.

JIM. Yeah. For now.

PAUL. Where does that word come from, anyway? Barista.

JIM. I'm not sure.

PAUL. It's Spanish. Right?

JIM. I think so.

PAUL. Are you Spanish?

JIM. No.

PAUL. Where are you from?

JIM. Long Island.

PAUL. No. I mean…you know…who are your people?

JIM. Who are my people?

PAUL. What's your background?

JIM. I'm Irish.

PAUL. Get the fuck out of here.

JIM. What?

PAUL. You are not Irish.

JIM. I am.

PAUL. What's your last name?

JIM. Kelly.

PAUL. Fuck off.

JIM. What?

PAUL. Fuck off.

JIM. What?

(**PAUL** *stares at* **JIM** *for a moment.*)

PAUL. You don't look Irish.

JIM. I'm black Irish.

PAUL. You look more…like…

JIM. More like what?

PAUL. You don't look Irish.

(**PAUL** *takes out his Blackberry and sends another message. He chuckles to himself.*)

So where is this Starbucks?

JIM. Sorry?

PAUL. The Starbucks. Where is it?

JIM. It's over on Madison.

PAUL. Madison and what?

JIM. Madison and seventy-fifth.

PAUL. So this is kind of your morning ritual before work. *(pause)* You have your egg and cheese, enjoy the scenery…

JIM. I don't know if I would call it a ritual.

PAUL. No? *(long pause)* This isn't a ritual?

JIM. Not really.

PAUL. But you do come here in the morning. I mean, you do regularly come here…to this bench…

(*Long pause. They stare at each other.*)

JIM. I guess I've been here before.

PAUL. You guess? *(long pause)* I always get confused when people say that.

JIM. What?

PAUL. "I guess."

JIM. I guess?

PAUL. Yes. *(pause)* It confuses me. I mean, if it's something that you do…or you did do…or you have done…I mean, your answer should just be yes…or no. Yes?

JIM. Uhm…Yes.

PAUL. Let me ask you something. You see the building across the street?

JIM. Yes.

PAUL. That is where I work. I work in that building.

JIM. OK.

PAUL. Do you know what goes on in that building?

JIM. No.

PAUL. I'll give you a clue. Do you see that big flag hanging from the façade?

JIM. Yes.

PAUL. It has something to do with that flag. *(pause)* Do you recognize that flag?

JIM. No.

PAUL. Really? That flag doesn't look familiar?

JIM. No.

PAUL. Come on, Jim. You seem like a bright guy. You do not recognize that flag?

JIM. Uhm. *(long pause)* Is it Turkey?

PAUL. Give the man a prize. Yes. It's the Turkish Embassy.

JIM. You work at the Turkish Embassy?

PAUL. Yes.

JIM. Are you Turkish?

PAUL. Do I look fucking Turkish, Jim?

JIM. No.

PAUL. I'm Irish, Jim. Just like you.

JIM. Oh.

PAUL. Unless you're not telling the truth.

JIM. Why would I lie about being Irish?

PAUL. I don't know. I mean, you said this egg and cheese on the bench thing was not a ritual, right?

JIM. Right.

(**PAUL** *stares at* **JIM** *for a few moments.*)

PAUL. Listen, Jim. I'm going to tell you something. OK? *(pause)* I'm really not so crazy about these Turks, but I'm sort of their security guy, and they are a very nervous bunch. *(pause)* Do you know why they're nervous?

JIM. No.

PAUL. Some people would say that they have a lot of blood on their hands.

JIM. Blood?

PAUL. Yeah. There are some people who really don't like the Turks.

JIM. Really?

PAUL. Have you heard of the Armenian Thing?

JIM. The Armenian *thing*?

PAUL. Yes. It happened a long time ago, but...how can I put this...some *things* tend to resonate. *(pause)*

JIM. They resonate?

PAUL. Yeah. Some things just...they resonate. You know? *(long pause)* If you had any idea how many hours I've spent watching videotape of you eating egg sandwiches. Jesus. *(pause)* You're OK, though. You're OK.

(**PAUL** *stands and takes a few deep breaths. He looks at the sky.*)

But listen, from now on, this bench is off limits, OK? *(pause)* You're making the Turks nervous.

(**PAUL** *does a few final stretches. He straightens his tie and brushes off his pants.*)

OK?

JIM. OK.

PAUL. Good. Now where did you say that Starbucks is?

JIM. Uhm. Madison and 75th.

PAUL. Right. I'm going to come down there one of these days for an Americano. OK?

JIM. OK.

PAUL. An iced Americano. *(pause)* God, I love this weather.

*(**PAUL** walks offstage left. **JIM** remains on the bench. He stares across the street. After a few moments, he stands and puts on his backpack. He remains standing there, staring across the street.)*

(blackout)

THE MERRY-GO-ROUND

CAST OF CHARACTERS

CLAIRE: In her twenties.
PHIL: In his twenties.

(*AT RISE: A typical motel room somewhere in suburban America.* **CLAIRE** *lies diagonally on a rumpled bed centerstage. She wears a bathrobe and her hair is wet. She stares up at the ceiling. There is a dresser with a mirror stage right. Next to the dresser, there is a video camera on a tripod. A door to the bathroom is stage left. It is slightly ajar and the sound of a man humming to himself in the shower can be heard. After a few moments, the shower stops and* **PHIL** *enters the room with a white towel around his waist.*)

PHIL. I like your work.

CLAIRE. Oh, thanks.

(**PHIL** *goes to the dresser. He takes a tube of hair product from a bag and begins working it into his hair.* **CLAIRE** *sits up and faces him.*)

PHIL. Are you joining the crew?

CLAIRE. I don't know.

PHIL. They ordered lunch from Vinny's.

CLAIRE. Vinny's?

PHIL. Yeah. The place across from the mall.

CLAIRE. OK. Which mall?

PHIL. The one near exit six…off the Interstate.

CLAIRE. Exit six…

PHIL. The big one.

CLAIRE. The big exit?

PHIL. No. The big mall.

CLAIRE. The big one…

PHIL. Yeah. Near exit six.

CLAIRE. The one with the ride? The horses?

PHIL. The horses.

CLAIRE. Yeah. What's it called? The ride with the horses.

PHIL. Horses?

CLAIRE. Fuck. What is it called?

PHIL. Oh. Yes. I know what you mean.

CLAIRE. The thing with the horses…

PHIL. Right. It spins around.

CLAIRE. Yeah. What the fuck is it called?

PHIL. Shit. Yes.

CLAIRE. You know what I mean. Right?

PHIL. Yes. Shit.

CLAIRE. Fuck.

PHIL. It's a…uhm…

CLAIRE. It's not a ferris wheel.

PHIL. No.

CLAIRE. It's not a…shit…what's the other thing?

PHIL. What?

CLAIRE. You know. That playground thing. You lie on it. It spins.

PHIL. Oh right. It has like…the bars.

CLAIRE. Yes.

PHIL. Other kids spin it.

CLAIRE. Yes. Yes.

PHIL. Other kids run around in a circle…holding the bar…pushing…

CLAIRE. Right.

PHIL. What *is* that thing called?

CLAIRE. I totally forget.

PHIL. Shit. Well, it's not that thing.

CLAIRE. You don't see those things in malls.

PHIL. No. You don't.

CLAIRE. This is the ride with the horses.

(**PHIL** *takes out some moisturizer and begins spreading it over his chest.* **CLAIRE** *takes some mascara from a make-up bag and begins applying it.*)

PHIL. Merry-go-round.

CLAIRE. Yes! Thank you. A merry-go-round.

PHIL. Thank god.

CLAIRE. A merry-go-round.

PHIL. A merry-go-round.

CLAIRE. Yes. With the horses.

PHIL. Yes. And the ring.

CLAIRE. The ring?

PHIL. Yeah. The ring. The brass ring.

CLAIRE. I don't remember that.

PHIL. You don't remember the ring?

CLAIRE. No.

PHIL. Maybe the ring was something else.

(**CLAIRE** *puts away her mascara and begins applying lipstick.*)

CLAIRE. You know, I totally forget what we were talking about.

PHIL. Um…what *were* we talking about?

CLAIRE. No fucking clue.

(**PHIL** *walks over to the window and looks out.*)

PHIL. What do you think of Donny?

CLAIRE. Donny?

(**PHIL** *turns to her.*)

PHIL. Yeah.

CLAIRE. What do I think of him?

PHIL. Yeah.

CLAIRE. I think he's nice.

PHIL. Yeah?

CLAIRE. Why?

PHIL. I don't know. Just wondering.

CLAIRE. You don't like him?

PHIL. No. I like him.

CLAIRE. Do you think he's weird?

PHIL. Yeah. Kind of.

CLAIRE. He's nicer than Louis Brown. Have you worked with Louis Brown?

PHIL. Yes. That guy is fucked up.

CLAIRE. I did this blow job thing with him a few years ago.

PHIL. Yeah. So did I.

CLAIRE. It was called like…Oral…something.

PHIL. *Oral Exams.*

CLAIRE. Right. Exactly. *Oral Exams.*

PHIL. Yeah. I worked on *Oral Exams.*

CLAIRE. You worked on *Oral Exams*?

PHIL. Yes. *Oral Exams 4.*

CLAIRE. OK. I worked on the first one.

PHIL. Right.

CLAIRE. I think he won an AVN award for it.

PHIL. Best blow job series.

CLAIRE. Right. Anyway, he totally freaked out on this guy.

PHIL. I'm not surprised.

CLAIRE. He freaked out.

PHIL. He's a nut-job.

CLAIRE. This sweet kid…totally new to the business… showed up late to set.

PHIL. Brown is a freak.

CLAIRE. The kid was like ten minutes late.

PHIL. He's such an ass-hole.

CLAIRE. …and Louis starts yelling at the kid…calling him a little fag.

PHIL. He's such an ass-hole.

CLAIRE. The kid starts crying.

PHIL. Really?

CLAIRE. He's bawling his eyes out.

PHIL. Christ.

CLAIRE. The kid's sitting on the edge of the bed…Frank Cipriani is there…behind the camera.

PHIL. Cipriani is another jerk.

CLAIRE. I hate that guy.

PHIL. He's a jerk.

CLAIRE. What is it with the camera guys in this business?

PHIL. I don't know. They're all jerks.

CLAIRE. So Louis is screaming at this kid. Cipriani is laughing. The lights are like a million degrees.

PHIL. Shit.

CLAIRE. I'm lying on the bed in this like latex bodysuit.

PHIL. Jesus.

CLAIRE. I feel like I'm in a microwave.

PHIL. Jesus Christ.

CLAIRE. And the kid is sitting there on the edge of the bed…naked…his whole body is red.

PHIL. His body's red?

CLAIRE. Yeah. It's like he's blushing. His whole body is blushing.

PHIL. Christ.

CLAIRE. And he's fucking bawling.

PHIL. Wow.

CLAIRE. What a prick.

PHIL. Yes.

CLAIRE. I'm just glad he's not directing this thing.

PHIL. I know.

CLAIRE. Donny's OK.

PHIL. Donny is good.

(**PHIL** *turns and looks out the window.*)

PHIL. I think the food is here.

CLAIRE. Oh yeah?

PHIL. Yeah. *(pause)* Oh. Vinny's.

CLAIRE. Vinny's?

PHIL. That's the place they ordered from.

CLAIRE. Oh.

PHIL. That's how we started talking about that ride…with the horses.

CLAIRE. Oh. Right.

PHIL. The…uhm…shit…what's it called again?

CLAIRE. The merry-go-round.

PHIL. Right. The merry-go-round.

CLAIRE. Right.

PHIL. Right.

(blackout)

COMMUNION

CAST OF CHARACTERS

ABBIE: In her fifties.
JIM: In his fifties. Abbie's husband.
NURSE: Offstage voice.

(*AT RISE:* **JIM** *reclines in a hospital bed at centerstage. His head and back are raised. His hospital gown has come untied and barely covers him. He looks weak and haggard. Stage left of the bed there is a table cluttered with newspapers, several half drunk strawberry milkshakes, scissors, medical tape, a bag of chips, pens and pencils, a note pad and a phone. An I.V. stand is on the other side of the bed. A bag of fluid is dripping into him. He has a nurse button close by. He has a newspaper in his hand, but his head is back and his eyes are closed.* **ABBIE**, *his wife, enters from stage right carrying a grocery bag and a sandwich. She looks tired and disheveled.*)

ABBIE. Hey, what are you doing?

JIM. What?

ABBIE. What are you doing still in bed?

JIM. Where the hell have you been?

ABBIE. You know where I've been.

JIM. I have no idea where you've been.

(**JIM** *notices how exposed he is and pulls a sheet over himself.*)

ABBIE. Think, Jim.

JIM. I have no idea. How am I supposed to know?

ABBIE. I went to the deli.

JIM. What deli?

ABBIE. The one across the street.

(**ABBIE** *removes a bottle of soda and a few packs of gum from the bag. She puts them on the bedside table.*)

JIM. The Dairy Barn?

ABBIE. No. The Dairy Barn is in Hudson.

JIM. Hudson?

ABBIE. Yes. Hudson…where we live.

JIM. We live in Hudson?

ABBIE. Yes, Jim. You're not thinking straight.

JIM. I thought we lived in Vermont.

ABBIE. We used to live in Vermont…a long time ago.

JIM. Jesus. Are you sure?

ABBIE. Yes. You need to think. You're confused.

JIM. Did you grab me a milkshake?

ABBIE. You have three milkshakes right there.

(*JIM looks over at the milkshakes. He picks one of them up and sips it.*)

JIM. It's melted.

ABBIE. Well, that's what happens when you leave it sitting there all morning.

JIM. Will you get me a fresh one, Abbie? I can't drink this.

ABBIE. No. I've gotten you three milkshakes already. Just drink what you have.

JIM. Jesus Christ. I can't drink this. It's fucking melted.

ABBIE. It's not melted.

JIM. It is.

ABBIE. No it is not.

JIM. Well, it's not thick. I like it thick.

ABBIE. I don't care.

JIM. Oh, nice. Thanks a lot. Here I am wasting away…

ABBIE. Boo-hoo-hoo. Stop being a baby and get washed up.

JIM. What?

ABBIE. Get out of that bed and get into the bathroom. You look terrible.

JIM. I have a better idea. Why don't you get your ass to the Dairy Barn and get me a large strawberry milkshake… and the *Times*.

ABBIE. It is NOT the Dairy Barn. The Dairy Barn is in Hudson.

JIM. Really? It's in Hudson?

ABBIE. You have three milkshakes right next to you and the *Times* is in your hand.

(**JIM** *looks at the newspaper in his hand. He unfolds it and looks at the date. He puts his hand to his head.*)

JIM. Jesus Christ. I am out of it.

(**ABBIE** *begins tugging at his sheet.*)

ABBIE. Let's go. You need to clean up.

JIM. Do NOT do that.

ABBIE. You are getting out of this bed right now.

JIM. Do not do that.

(**ABBIE** *tugs harder on the sheet.*)

ABBIE. Get up.

JIM. Get your hands off me, woman.

ABBIE. You look like crap, Jim.

JIM. Well, I feel like crap.

ABBIE. You need to wash up.

JIM. I am not getting out of this bed.

ABBIE. Father Mike will be here to give you communion in a half an hour.

JIM. What the fuck are you talking about?

ABBIE. Father Mike is coming to give you communion.

JIM. Who the fuck is Father Mike?

ABBIE. I'm not going through this with you again.

(**ABBIE** *rips the sheet off of him.* **JIM** *grabs the nurse button that is attached to the wall by a cord.*)

JIM. You get your hands off me, woman. You get your fucking hands off me.

ABBIE. Put down the nurse button.

JIM. I will not. Now, back off!

ABBIE. Drop it.

JIM. Get the hell out of here. Go get me a shake.

ABBIE. Drop the nurse button.

JIM. Get me a damn milkshake, woman.

ABBIE. I swear, Jim, if you disturb those poor nurses one more time, I am going to rip that thing out of the wall.

JIM. I will have you removed from this room if you do not back off.

(**ABBIE** *grabs his ankles.* **JIM** *screams and presses the button. A bell rings once and a red light goes on behind the bed.*)

ABBIE. Jim! You stop it with that button. The nurses have more important things to do than…

(*The* **NURSE**'s *voice comes from a speaker behind* **JIM**'s *bed*)

NURSE. *(offstage)* Yes?

JIM. I need some help, please.

NURSE. *(offstage)* Are you in pain, Jim?

JIM. Yes. It's my wife. She is abusing me.

ABBIE. Sorry Marie. Don't listen to him. He's just being a jerk.

NURSE. *(offstage)* Oh. OK then. You stop being a jerk Jim.

(**ABBIE** *grabs the nurse button out of* **JIM**'s *hand and drops it behind the bed where he can't reach it.*)

JIM. You give me that fucking button.

(**ABBIE** *grabs him by the wrists and begins pulling him out of the bed.*)

Jesus Christ, Abbie. Get the fuck off me.

ABBIE. No. I will not. You are getting in that shower right now.

(**ABBIE** *forces him out of the bed. He's on his feet now with his arms around her neck, holding on for balance, but still fighting her.*)

JIM. You get the fuck off me, woman. You get the fuck away from me.

ABBIE. I will not.

JIM. Jesus, I'm in pain. I'M IN PAIN!

ABBIE. I do not care. Do you hear me? I do not care!

(**JIM**'s *legs begin to buckle.* **ABBIE** *tries dragging him, but he's heavy and she struggles to keep him up.*)

ABBIE. Stand up, Jim!

JIM. I am standing up.

ABBIE. Stop bending your knees.

JIM. I can't help it. It fucking hurts.

(They collapse to the floor.)

Abbie. Sweetheart. I'm in so much pain.

*(**JIM** and **ABBIE** are on the floor. He still has his arms around her neck. **ABBIE** has dropped her head onto his shoulder. She surrenders.)*

ABBIE. I don't care.

JIM. Jesus. I'm so fucked up. *(pause)* I'm so fucked up right now.

ABBIE. I don't care.

JIM. Please get me a milkshake.

ABBIE. No.

JIM. Come on, baby.

ABBIE. No.

JIM. Come on, Abbie. Stop it.

ABBIE. I don't care.

JIM. Jesus Christ, Abbie. Please. *(pause)* Please.

*(**JIM** pulls her close to him.)*

(blackout)

THE MONSTER

CAST OF CHARACTERS

LOU: In his sixties.
SPENCER: In his thirties.

THE MONSTER was first presented at the 34th Samuel French Off-Off Broadway Short Play Festival at Playwrights Horizons Theatre on July 18th, 2009. The Producer was Jessica Greer Morris. The performance was directed by Eric Michael Gillett. The Production Stage Manager was Russ Weatherford. The cast was as follows:

LOU . . . . Richard O'Brien
SPENCER. . . . . Giorgio Litt

(AT RISE: A red Ducati motorcycle leans on its kickstand at centerstage. A salesman, **LOU**, *is polishing the tank with a special cloth. He is wearing a charcoal suit, a white shirt and a red tie.* **SPENCER** *enters from stage right. He is wearing khakis and a blue shirt. He stops and looks at the bike.)*

LOU. Easy on the eyes, eh?

SPENCER. Yes. Beautiful.

LOU. Beautiful, but dangerous.

SPENCER. Beautiful, but dangerous. Yes.

LOU. The Ducati Monster.

SPENCER. Very nice.

LOU. Six hundred and ninety six cubic centimeters of 'kaboom.'

SPENCER. 'Kaboom.'

LOU. Not for the faint of heart.

SPENCER. No.

*(***LOU*** points to the engine.)*

LOU. Newly designed Adler Power Torque Clutch.

SPENCER. Sweet.

LOU. Desmodromic valve system.

SPENCER. Desmo?

LOU. Desmodromic. Eliminates the spring.

SPENCER. Oh.

LOU. Perfect valve timing.

SPENCER. Really?

LOU. Pardon my français, but fucking really.

SPENCER. It's so…

LOU. Muscular?

SPENCER. Yes. Exactly. Muscular.

LOU. It's totally pumped.

SPENCER. Right.

LOU. It's ripped.

SPENCER. Completely.

LOU. It's big boned.

> (**SPENCER** *looks puzzled for a moment.* **LOU** *grins and puts his hand on* **SPENCER***'s shoulder.*)

How do you take your coffee?

SPENCER. Oh, I'm fine.

LOU. Milk?

SPENCER. I'm good. Really.

LOU. Sugar?

SPENCER. Seriously. I just had a coffee.

LOU. It's Italian roast. Freshly brewed. A small cup.

SPENCER. Do you have half and half?

LOU. Mais, oui.

SPENCER. And Splenda.

LOU. Done. Feel free to mount the monster.

> (**LOU** *walks offstage left.* **SPENCER** *steps around the motorcycle. He bends down to look closely at the engine. He stands for a moment before climbing on. He leans down like a racer.* **LOU** *returns with a cup of coffee and a sleek looking helmet.* **SPENCER** *lifts his leg to dismount.*)

Don't get off. I'm going to show you something.

> (**LOU** *hands the helmet to* **SPENCER**. *He puts the coffee down on the floor and pulls out his camera phone. He stands back and points it at* **SPENCER**.)

OK. Put on the helmet and get into that racing position.

SPENCER. Put on the helmet?

> (**LOU** *does not respond. He stands with the camera phone pointing at* **SPENCER**. **SPENCER** *puts on the helmet and gets into a racing pose. The camera phone clicks a picture.*)

LOU. Oh man, you've got to see this.

(**SPENCER** *moves to get off the bike.*)

No. Stay on. I'll send it to you. Give me your number.

SPENCER. That's OK. Really.

LOU. 212?

SPENCER. 917.

LOU. 917...

SPENCER. It's 917-388-4771.

LOU. Ok. *(pause)* There we go.

(**SPENCER***'s cell phone begins to ring, and he pulls it out of his pocket. He lifts the visor of the helmet and looks at the photo.*)

SPENCER. Nice.

LOU. You've got good form. Do you still race?

(**SPENCER** *gets off the bike and stands next to* **LOU**.*)*

SPENCER. Race?

LOU. I'm assuming you've raced before.

(**SPENCER** *removes the helmet and puts it on the seat of the motorcycle.* **SPENCER** *picks up the coffee and hands it to him.*)

SPENCER. No. Never.

LOU. You could've fooled me. You have perfect form.

SPENCER. Wow.

(**LOU** *extends his hand.*)

LOU. Lou Schwebber.

(**SPENCER** *shakes his hand.*)

SPENCER. Spencer Wilson.

LOU. So, you've never raced.

SPENCER. Never.

LOU. But you've ridden.

SPENCER. No. Well, kind of.

LOU. There is no kind of, Spencer.

SPENCER. I rented a scooter in Bermuda a few years ago.

LOU. Here at Ducati, we don't really recognize the scooter.

(**SPENCER** *slowly walks around the bike. He leans down and looks closely at the tires.*)

Have you looked at our other models?

SPENCER. No.

LOU. The Multistrada is our other big seller.

SPENCER. I think I'm pretty set on the Monster.

LOU. You have good taste.

(**SPENCER** *continues inspecting the bike.* **LOU** *watches him. There is a long silence.*)

Are you sure you've never ridden?

SPENCER. Never. Just in Bermuda. The scooter.

LOU. Well, I think the Monster really suits you.

SPENCER. Yeah. *(pause)* A buddy of mine had this great poster of one. That's really the first time I saw the Monster.

LOU. Did your friend actually own one, or did he just have the poster?

SPENCER. He had a real one *and* the poster.

LOU. Oh, yeah?

SPENCER. I met him during my last tour in Iraq.

LOU. Oh. Wow.

SPENCER. His name was Anthony Monaco. A big guy from Brooklyn.

LOU. Cool. What part of Brooklyn?

SPENCER. Bensonhurst. *(pause)* I swear, all he talked about was Italian food and his Ducati Monster.

LOU. Two healthy obsessions.

SPENCER. Anthony Monaco. He was a great guy.

LOU. Of course. He was from Brooklyn.

SPENCER. Yeah. Bensonhurst, Brooklyn.

LOU. Fuhgettaboutit.

SPENCER. You want to hear something crazy?

LOU. Sure.

SPENCER. Anthony and I were at this Combat Outpost in Diyala.

LOU. Diyala. Yeah. I've heard of it.

SPENCER. We were at the front gates, standing watch, when we notice this motorcycle in the distance. It was coming toward us at a pretty good clip.

LOU. Sounds scary.

SPENCER. So we're watching this bike get closer. There are signs all along the road telling people to slow down, but this bike is just flying toward us.

LOU. Jesus. Did you have to shoot?

SPENCER. First we just fired some warning shots, but the bike just seemed to pick up speed.

LOU. Man. Sounds crazy.

SPENCER. So finally, we have no choice. I fire directly at this nutcase and he drops right down onto the handle bars.

LOU. Man.

SPENCER. He's like face down, slumped over the handlebars.

LOU. Jesus Christ.

SPENCER. But the fucking dude is still coming at us.

LOU. Are you serious?

SPENCER. The bike never lost its balance and the way he fell forward must have locked the throttle because that bike was not slowing down.

LOU. That's unbelievable.

SPENCER. It was fucking crazy. So, we fired some more shots, but the wind was kicking up dust. We couldn't get a clear shot.

LOU. Oh, man.

SPENCER. Anthony decides to run over to the edge of the road. Maybe he thought he could get a clearer shot or something. Anyway, this bike just comes flying up the road and Anthony finally gets a good shot and blows out the rear tire. *(pause)* But instead of going right down, the bike skids and veers right at him.

LOU. Oh, man.

SPENCER. It just nails him.

LOU. Oh, man.

SPENCER. I go running over to him. The bike's on his fucking chest.

LOU. Oh, man.

SPENCER. His face was just like…He was making this face. It was like he was sticking his tongue out. You know, like on purpose.

LOU. He was dead.

SPENCER. He was so fucking dead.

LOU. Jesus Christ.

SPENCER. Anthony Monaco. Fucking Brooklyn.

LOU. That is just…

SPENCER. It's fucking ironic.

LOU. It's sad.

SPENCER. It's sad and ironic.

LOU. It is a really screwed up war.

SPENCER. Yeah. It's a screwed up world.

LOU. Yeah.

*(**SPENCER** and **LOU** both stare at the bike. There is a long silence.)*

LOU. *(cont.)* Listen. I think you should take your time before you commit to the Monster.

SPENCER. You think I should take my time?

LOU. I think you should take a couple of days to think about it. Maybe take a week.

SPENCER. But I've already thought about this. I mean I know I want this bike.

LOU. Look, I'm just saying, I think it's always a good idea to give your self some time.

SPENCER. Really?

LOU. I'm just thinking that the Monster's a powerful bike, and if you've never ridden, you may want to start with something more…manageable. *(long pause)* Here's my card.

*(**LOU** hands **SPENCER** his card.)*

(blackout)

BASIC PLUMBING

CAST OF CHARACTERS

RUSSEL: In his forties
BRUCE: In his sixties

(AT RISE: The reference desk of a small town library is centerstage. It is clean, and well organized, with two computers, a wall clock, a box of pencils, and a bar code scanner. There is limited decoration aside from the usual library signage. **RUSSEL**, *the librarian, stands behind the desk, staring down at his computer screen. He is wearing khaki pants and a pale blue shirt. The sound of a man coughing turns his attention to stage left.)*

RUSSEL. Oh…Jesus.

*(***BRUCE*** enters from stage left. He has on a green ski hat, a bright yellow, down-filled vest over a ratty looking sweater and camouflage cargo shorts. He also has on a pair of furry boots. His knees are red. He is dusted with snow.* **BRUCE** *stops about six feet from the desk. There is a long silence while the two men stare at each other.)*

BRUCE. Snow's coming down fast.

RUSSEL. Oh yeah?

BRUCE. Yeah.

RUSSEL. Well, I'm just on my way out. Hope route 6 isn't too bad.

BRUCE. You should take 6A.

RUSSEL. You think?

BRUCE. I was just on 6. It's a mess.

RUSSEL. But don't they clear 6 more often than 6A?

*(***RUSSEL*** wraps a scarf around his neck and puts on his coat.)*

BRUCE. Sure, but there's more people on 6. It's a mess.

RUSSEL. Yes, well, it's a safe and orderly mess.

BRUCE. Civilization trumps the wilderness.

RUSSEL. Exactly.

BRUCE. Fuck-face.

RUSSEL. Excuse me?

(**RUSSEL** and **BRUCE** *just stare at each other for a moment. After shutting down the computers,* **RUSSEL** *takes his hat out of a drawer and puts it on. He looks at* **BRUCE**. *There is a silence.*)

BRUCE. I need a book.

RUSSEL. I'm sorry, but the library is closed.

BRUCE. You don't close until 8.

RUSSEL. That's right. It is 8.

BRUCE. It's 7:58.

RUSSEL. I lock the door at 8.

BRUCE. Right.

RUSSEL. The check out desk closes before that.

BRUCE. It's called "Basic Plumbing."

RUSSEL. I'm sorry, Bruce, but I just shut down the system. We are closed.

BRUCE. It's in the non-fiction aisle.

RUSSEL. I know where it is.

BRUCE. It has a red spine. Impossible to miss.

RUSSEL. Bruce, the book could be sitting right in front me. That's not the point.

BRUCE. What's the point?

RUSSEL. The system is shut down. I cannot process the transaction.

BRUCE. Fuck the system. We'll write it out.

RUSSEL. No.

BRUCE. I'll sign a form. We'll do it old school.

RUSSEL. Listen, Bruce, we open at 9 tomorrow morning. Why don't you come back tomorrow?

BRUCE. It's the shitter.

RUSSEL. What?

BRUCE. My shitter. It's messed up.

RUSSEL. Maybe you should call a professional. A real plumber.

BRUCE. Maybe you should get the book, fuck-face.

RUSSEL. I'm leaving now, Bruce.

BRUCE. Fucking prick. Fucking Prius-driving, route 6 motherfucker. *(pause)* Fuck-face.

RUSSEL. Bruce, I am leaving now, and if you…

BRUCE. My shitter is out of order. I need that book.

RUSSEL. Call a plumber.

BRUCE. There's a blizzard out there! It's dark out and there's a blizzard!

RUSSEL. That's not my problem.

BRUCE. Sharon would have just got the book.

RUSSEL. What?

BRUCE. Sharon would have just got the book. She would have just handed me the book. No hassles.

RUSSEL. No, she wouldn't have

BRUCE. Yes, she would.

RUSSEL. If Sharon was closing up for the night I can tell you that she would not have given you the book. She would have asked you to come back in the morning.

BRUCE. No way.

RUSSEL. Yes way.

BRUCE. No way.

RUSSEL. Bruce. She would not have given you the book. You know how I know?

BRUCE. Yes, she would.

RUSSEL. You know how I know?

BRUCE. She liked me.

RUSSEL. You know how I know she would not have given you the book, Bruce?

BRUCE. Because you're an asshole?

RUSSEL. No. It's because you tried this with her many times.

BRUCE. Fuck you.

RUSSEL. You tried this over and over with her, and every time she told you the same thing. She told you exactly what I'm telling you. She told you to come back in the morning.

BRUCE. She and I had a connection.

RUSSEL. A connection?

BRUCE. Sharon and I understood each other.

RUSSEL. Bruce, I am leaving now.

BRUCE. Sharon was a beautiful woman.

RUSSEL. I'm leaving now Bruce.

BRUCE. Sharon was a very beautiful woman.

RUSSEL. I know, Bruce. Sharon was very beautiful.

BRUCE. I loved Sharon.

RUSSEL. I'm leaving now Bruce.

BRUCE. When Sharon gets back from India, this place will be good again.

RUSSEL. Bruce. *(pause)* When Sharon gets back from India, she's going to go to school in Maine.

BRUCE. Maine?

RUSSEL. Yes.

BRUCE. She's moving to Maine?

RUSSEL. Yes. To do her Master's Degree.

BRUCE. Her Master's Degree?

RUSSEL. Yes. Her MFA. *(pause)* Her Master's in Fine Arts.

BRUCE. Fuck you.

RUSSEL. It's a writing program.

BRUCE. Fuck you.

RUSSEL. Poetry. She'll be writing poetry.

BRUCE. Fuck you. *(long pause)* Well, she'll be back in the summer. She'll work in the summer.

RUSSEL. I'm leaving now, Bruce.

BRUCE. Do you think she'll be back in the summer?

RUSSEL. No. I think she'll stay in Maine.

BRUCE. What the fuck is in Maine?

RUSSEL. I'm leaving now, Bruce.

(**RUSSEL** *buttons his coat and puts on a pair of woolen mits.* **BRUCE** *watches him.*)

BRUCE. You taking 6?

RUSSEL. Yes.

BRUCE. It's a mess.

RUSSEL. I know, but I need to stop for gas.

BRUCE. Okay. Be careful out there.

> (**BRUCE** *turns and leaves.* **RUSSEL** *clears some things off the desk and walks toward the exit. He stops. There is a pause. He turns and disappears off stage right only to reemerge carrying a book with a red spine. He exits quickly to catch* **BRUCE**.)
>
> (*blackout*)

THE DRIVING RANGE

CAST OF CHARACTERS

DAVE: In his twenties
CHRISTINE: In her forties

(AT RISE: Three identical golf bags – each with a full set of gleaming clubs – stand alone on a bright carpet of short green grass. The first bag is stage left, the second at center, and the third stage right. A large basket of golf balls sits next to each bag. An electric golf cart, driven by a Red Rock Golf Resort employee, enters from stage right with two passengers. **DAVE** *steps off the back seat and goes to the center bag. He is wearing a Red Rock Resort golf shirt and khaki pants. He begins inspecting the clubs.* **CHRISTINE** *gets off the cart and stands watching him. She wears a golf skirt and top that look brand new. A tag still hangs from the back of her skirt. The cart exits stage left.)*

CHRISTINE. What I admire most about this place is the way every need is anticipated.

*(***DAVE*** *takes a handful of white tees from the bag and scatters them on the grass.)*

DAVE. How do you mean?

CHRISTINE. Well, look at all this fine equipment here…just waiting for us.

DAVE. It's pretty standard at these golf resorts, actually.

CHRISTINE. Really?

DAVE. It's all about keeping things organized.

*(***CHRISTINE*** *walks over to the golf bag at stage left.)*

CHRISTINE. Is that it?

DAVE. That's about it.

CHRISTINE. Well, that's very nice. *(pause)* Will I be using these clubs?

DAVE. Yeah. You can feel them out if you'd like.

CHRISTINE. Feel them out?

*(***DAVE*** *looks over at her and there's an awkward silence.)*

DAVE. You can just swing a couple of them…see how they feel.

(CHRISTINE takes out the driver and swings it slowly in the air like a baseball bat. DAVE removes a few irons from his bag and lays them in a geometric formation on the grass. He continues to set up the area for his lesson.)

CHRISTINE. This one feels pretty good.

DAVE. That's the driver.

CHRISTINE. The driver…

DAVE. You'll use that club to drive the ball onto the fairway.

CHRISTINE. OK.

DAVE. It's the power club. It gives you distance.

CHRISTINE. The power club…I like that.

DAVE. We won't be using that one today.

CHRISTINE. No? No power club?

DAVE. No power club.

CHRISTINE. But, I like the power club.

DAVE. Today we'll be focusing on the irons.

CHRISTINE. Really? Just the irons?

DAVE. Just the irons.

CHRISTINE. No driver?

DAVE. Not today.

CHRISTINE. Not just a little driver?

DAVE. Today, it's all irons.

(CHRISTINE puts the driver back into the bag and walks over to DAVE.)

CHRISTINE. You know, I think we forgot an introduction.

(DAVE looks up from his preparations. He has just put on a white golf glove. He puts out his hand.)

DAVE. Dave.

CHRISTINE. Christine.

(There is an awkward pause.)

So, the lesson begins.

DAVE. Right.

*(**DAVE** takes a pitching wedge out of his bag.)*

We're going to start out with some basic swing mechanics.

CHRISTINE. Sounds good to me.

DAVE. I want you to watch me swing this club.

CHRISTINE. OK.

DAVE. Tell me what you see.

CHRISTINE. What I see?

DAVE. What you notice…about my swing.

CHRISTINE. OK.

*(**DAVE** puts his head down and slowly brings the club back over his head and then swings the club slowly around in one smooth motion. He looks up at **CHRISTINE**.)*

DAVE. So. Did you notice anything?

CHRISTINE. I noticed that you brought the club back over your head.

DAVE. Very good.

CHRISTINE. And then you swung the club around in a full circle.

DAVE. Good. Anything else?

CHRISTINE. I don't think so.

DAVE. OK. I want you to swing the club now.

(He hands her the club. She takes it and feels the weight of it in her hand.)

CHRISTINE. It's heavy.

DAVE. You think?

CHRISTINE. It's heavier than the driver.

DAVE. It's made with heavier materials.

CHRISTINE. But the driver is more powerful, right?

DAVE. That's right.

CHRISTINE. And it's bigger…much bigger.

DAVE. It is a bigger club.

CHRISTINE. So, shouldn't it be more…

DAVE. In golf, it's not really about weight. It's about the size and shape of the club.

CHRISTINE. OK.

DAVE. And the length of the shaft.

CHRISTINE. Oh.

DAVE. And the material.

CHRISTINE. The material.

DAVE. Yeah…what it's made of…the actual material.

CHRISTINE. I see. Interesting.

(They stand quietly for a moment. CHRISTINE places her hands together on the club handle and gets into position.)

This doesn't feel right.

DAVE. OK. Your grip is a bit off. Here, relax your hands.

*(**DAVE** kneels down and begins adjusting her grip. He moves her hands and fingers into place.)*

Relax your hands.

CHRISTINE. I am.

DAVE. I mean relax them more.

CHRISTINE. I don't want to drop the club.

DAVE. You won't.

*(She relaxes her hands and **DAVE** continues to set her fingers in place. She watches him.)*

OK. That's it.

CHRISTINE. That's the grip?

DAVE. That is the grip.

CHRISTINE. It feels strange.

DAVE. You'll get used to it.

CHRISTINE. What next?

DAVE. Turn around and get into a comfortable position.

*(**CHRISTINE** turns and stands with her back to **DAVE**. She holds the club out in front of her.)*

CHRISTINE. Like this?

DAVE. Is that comfortable?

CHRISTINE. Not really

DAVE. OK. Do whatever you need to do to be comfortable.

*(**CHRISTINE** lets her shoulder and back relax. The head of the club comes down and rests in the grass.)*

CHRISTINE. OK.

DAVE. You're comfortable?

CHRISTINE. Yes.

DAVE. Alright. Go ahead and swing the club.

*(**CHRISTINE** lifts the club behind her head and swings it in a full circle around her body.)*

CHRISTINE. How was that?

DAVE. That was very good.

CHRISTINE. It felt pretty good.

DAVE. Now, I want you to get back into that first position.

CHRISTINE. OK.

DAVE. And I want you to relax again.

*(**CHRISTINE**'s shoulders drop and the club lowers.)*

CHRISTINE. OK.

*(**DAVE** steps closer to her and kneels down. He looks at her legs.)*

DAVE. I'm going to re-position your feet.

CHRISTINE. OK.

*(**DAVE** puts his hands on her calves.)*

DAVE. Now, move your left foot out a bit more.

CHRISTINE. Like this?

DAVE. Perfect. Now move your other foot out.

CHRISTINE. OK.

*(**DAVE** notices the tag. He takes it in his hand and reads it.)*

DAVE. Would you like me to remove this?

CHRISTINE. What?

DAVE. The tag is still on your skirt.

(**CHRISTINE** *looks back over her shoulder.*)

CHRISTINE. Oh my god. That's embarrassing.

DAVE. Do you want it off?

CHRISTINE. If you don't mind. Do you have any scissors?

DAVE. No.

CHRISTINE. Well, just try not to rip the fabric.

(**DAVE** *pulls at the tag carefully. When this fails, he brings the tag to his mouth and bites down on the piece of plastic.* **CHRISTINE** *remains in her position, with her head facing forward. A few moments pass.*)

Any luck?

DAVE. No.

CHRISTINE. Let me try.

(**CHRISTINE** *reaches behind her and fumbles for the tag. She finds it and pulls it around. As she pulls at it,* **DAVE** *remains kneeling behind her. He stares at the pink underwear that is suddenly in full view.* **CHRISTINE** *continues fumbling with the tag.*)

Don't you hate these tags?

DAVE. Yes.

CHRISTINE. Like why are there always three or four tags on everything.

DAVE. I don't know.

(**CHRISTINE** *finally snaps off the tag. She tosses it onto the grass and lets go of her skirt. Her underwear disappears from view.*)

CHRISTINE. OK. Back to business.

(**DAVE** *puts his hands on her calves again.*)

DAVE. You want to keep your feet shoulder width apart.

CHRISTINE. Shoulder width apart. OK.

DAVE. Now swing the club.

(**CHRISTINE** *swings the club again.*)

(*blackout*)

BEHIND THE WHEEL

CAST OF CHARACTERS

ADAM: In his forties
BEN: In his forties

(*AT RISE: Books line the walls of a dimly lit study.* **BEN** *reclines on a leather couch, stage left. He has a glass of scotch resting on his chest and his eyes are closed. After a few moments, the door opens, upstage right, and* **ADAM** *enters. He pulls a chair to the center of the room and sits.*)

ADAM. Hey doc. *(pause)* Hey. Doctor.

BEN. The doctor is not in.

ADAM. Wake up.

BEN. I am up.

ADAM. Wake up.

BEN. I'm up.

(**BEN** *opens his eyes and sits up on the couch. He stares at* **ADAM** *for a moment.*)

What's going on down there?

ADAM. The usual Thanksgiving chaos.

BEN. Is Mom alright?

ADAM. She seems fine.

BEN. I worry about her.

ADAM. You shouldn't.

(**BEN** *finishes his drink and leans back on the couch. There is a long pause.*)

BEN. I saw your father-in-law yesterday.

ADAM. Yes, Clara told me.

BEN. The man is a miracle.

ADAM. That's what everyone says.

BEN. He is a miracle.

(**ADAM** *walks over to the desk and takes an unopened bottle of scotch from a drawer. He holds it out.*)

ADAM. You mind?

BEN. No. Go ahead.

(**ADAM** *pours two big glasses of scotch, hands one to* **BEN**, *and sits on the couch.*)

ADAM. I actually wanted to talk to you about him. *(pause)* I appreciate the way you've taken care of him.

BEN. Come on, Adam. Are you kidding?

ADAM. Seriously. I mean, he's family.

BEN. Exactly. He's family.

ADAM. Well, look, I know it can be a bit awkward dealing with family.

BEN. It's been fine. He's a good patient. *(long pause)* How's Clara?

ADAM. She's OK. *(long pause)* It's weird, though.

BEN. What's weird?

ADAM. I don't know…the way the guy keeps going.

BEN. He's a miracle.

ADAM. I mean, we were ready to write him off.

BEN. I remember.

ADAM. It was exactly two years ago.

BEN. The man's a trouper.

ADAM. Clara's mom called in the kids from Chicago.

BEN. God. Right.

ADAM. I remember picking up Jenny from JFK. She cried the whole way to the hospital.

BEN. Jenny's nice. I like Jenny.

ADAM. I even bought a black suit at Daffy's. Can you believe that?

BEN. The man was at the end.

ADAM. Clara made this huge dinner, and we brought it to St. Lukes.

BEN. Right. That's right.

ADAM. Were you there?

BEN. No, but I remember you telling me about all the Tupperware.

ADAM. Yes, the Tupperware. *(pause)* We all sat around Bill's bed, eating turkey out of those blue plastic tubs.

BEN. Jesus.

ADAM. Bill was just laying there under a sheet…wheezing.

BEN. Jesus.

ADAM. He had that fluid in his lungs.

BEN. Pleural effusion.

ADAM. Pleural effusion. Right.

BEN. That was a rough time.

ADAM. It was so fucking rough.

BEN. The man's a miracle.

ADAM. They were ready to give up on him.

BEN. I know.

ADAM. Thanks to you, though…

BEN. Don't thank me.

ADAM. Come on. You got the ball rolling.

BEN. It wasn't me. The guy's a miracle.

ADAM. You made the call to take some action.

BEN. I drained the fluid.

ADAM. Right, you drained the fluid.

BEN. It was for his comfort.

ADAM. You saved him.

(**ADAM** *goes to the desk and picks up the bottle. He walks downstage and stares out toward the audience. He sips his drink. There is a long pause.*)

I need to talk to you about something.

BEN. OK.

ADAM. I'm not a happy person right now, Ben.

BEN. No?

ADAM. No. Things are a bit bleak right now.

BEN. Bleak?

ADAM. Things are bleak. I'm kind of in a tunnel right now.

BEN. A tunnel.

ADAM. Listen, I need to ask you to do something.

BEN. OK.

ADAM. It's a strange request. *(pause)* I don't want to ask you, but…

BEN. What is it?

ADAM. I need you to ease up on Bill.

BEN. You need me to ease up on Bill?

ADAM. Yes.

BEN. I'm not following you.

ADAM. I want you to stop being so…good.

BEN. Good?

ADAM. I want you to stop being so aggressive. You know, in your treatment of him.

BEN. You think I'm treating him too aggressively? Really?

ADAM. No. *(pause)* That's not really what I mean.

BEN. I've actually been pretty conservative.

ADAM. I know.

(**ADAM** *pulls the chair over to the couch and sits across from* **BEN.**)

Look, I know you are the one who sees this shit every day.

BEN. What shit?

ADAM. You know. Death.

BEN. Right.

ADAM. But I'm not sure you understand what it does to people. I mean what it really does.

BEN. Adam, I understand what it does to people.

ADAM. This man's recovery…it's destroying everything.

BEN. It's destroying everything?

(*Long pause.* **BEN** *gets up and grabs the bottle from the desk. He sits back down and pours.*)

Come on, Bro. Talk to me.

ADAM. It's hard to explain. It's like this man has become a black hole.

BEN. Well, the man is sick.

ADAM. No. He's not a sick man. He's a dying man. He's a dead man.

BEN. OK. He's a dying man.

ADAM. And dying men suck people into them.

BEN. You're going a bit far.

ADAM. No. I'm not.

BEN. Adam.

ADAM. You don't understand, OK?

BEN. Adam.

ADAM. This is not the stuff they train you for at medical school.

BEN. OK. Now you are just talking shit.

ADAM. The man has destroyed my marriage. *(pause)* For two years he has sucked the life out of my marriage.

BEN. The man has cancer.

ADAM. Fuck cancer, OK?

BEN. Adam…

ADAM. You don't understand. Everything is on hold. Everything has been darkened by him.

BEN. Have some compassion.

ADAM. I have lost my…

BEN. What? You have lost your what?

ADAM. I don't know.

BEN. You have lost your what?

ADAM. I have lost my power.

BEN. Your power?

ADAM. Yes.

BEN. What do you mean?

ADAM. You know what I mean.

BEN. I do not know what you mean.

ADAM. Listen. I am not like you. There are things I need.

BEN. There are things you need?

ADAM. I can't just hide in my office the way you do. I need to feel…I need to have an influence on things.

BEN. What are you saying? I don't hide in my office.

ADAM. Oh, come on, Ben. You have your books and your diplomas and your position at the hospital…

BEN. What the fuck are you saying?

ADAM. I'm saying that you are the kind of man who is important at work, but you're invisible in your own house.

BEN. That is ridiculous.

ADAM. It's true. It's a kind of trade off. Your lab coat is your power. At home, without it, you're just some guy who lives in your wife's house.

BEN. You are out of your mind.

ADAM. You see, when I go to work I am just some guy. I am zero. I can't afford to disappear at home.

BEN. You're out of your mind.

ADAM. And don't be confused. I am not trying to do my father-in-law any favors.

BEN. You're fucking drunk.

ADAM. I want you to let the man die.

BEN. He is dying.

ADAM. Let him die, Ben.

BEN. You're drunk.

ADAM. I want…I want to be the one…

BEN. You want to be the one?

ADAM. I want to be behind the wheel. Don't you understand?

BEN. No. I don't understand.

ADAM. I want to be behind the wheel. I want to have some control here. I…I…

BEN. No. Adam.

ADAM. I want you to stop helping him.

BEN. I'm his fucking doctor.

ADAM. Stop helping him.

BEN. Adam.

ADAM. Please.

BEN. No.

ADAM. Just let him die.

BEN. Adam. I will not.

ADAM. He's destroying everything.

BEN. Adam.

ADAM. He's killing everything. Please, Ben. Please. I'm in a dark place. I've lost Clara.

BEN. Adam…

ADAM. Please. I'm in a tunnel. *(pause)* Please. *(pause)* Save me.

(blackout)

THE INCLUSION

CAST OF CHARACTERS

CYNTHIA: In her forties
BILL: In his forties

(AT RISE: A small jewelry store in New York. A glass coffee table and two stylish chairs are center stage. A glass case is up from the table and chairs. **CYNTHIA** *stands behind the showcase. A variety of attractive pieces are on display. She is looking down at two diamonds that are laid out on a black piece of felt. She lifts one of them up with a pair of tweezers and looks at it through an eye piece. She puts it down gently and inspects the other. A bell rings.* **CYNTHIA** *looks up, as if at a security monitor, and then presses a button that buzzes the customer in.* **CYNTHIA** *takes a deep breath and quickly checks herself out in a mirror.* **BILL** *enters from stage right.)*

BILL. Cynthia Walsh.

CYNTHIA. Bill Hoffman.

BILL. Jesus Christ.

CYNTHIA. Jesus Christ.

BILL. This is really amazing.

CYNTHIA. Yes. It really is.

(There is a silence and then **BILL** *opens his arms.* **CYNTHIA** *comes around from behind the counter and embraces him. They kiss on both cheeks.)*

BILL. It is so great to see you.

CYNTHIA. I know. It's great to see you too. You look good.

BILL. You look fantastic. Really, just fantastic.

CYNTHIA. I like the double kiss.

BILL. Yeah, I haven't done that since college.

CYNTHIA. Me either.

BILL. But it just came so naturally.

CYNTHIA. Didn't it?

BILL. It really did.

CYNTHIA. Where the hell did we get that from anyway?

BILL. I have no idea.

CYNTHIA. I mean it's not like we were going to school in France.

BILL. I know.

CYNTHIA. It was Chicago.

BILL. Yes, but we were artists.

CYNTHIA. Oh, right.

BILL. Correction. We were posing as artists.

CYNTHIA. Yes. That is more accurate.

> (**CYNTHIA** *goes to the table and pulls back one of the chairs.*)

Please have a seat.

> (**BILL** *sits down.* **CYNTHIA** *goes to the glass case and picks up the black felt and the diamonds. She puts them down on the table.*)

I picked these two out for you.

> (**BILL** *leans over and looks down at the diamonds*)

BILL. They're beautiful.

CYNTHIA. Would you like something to drink?

BILL. Sure. What have you got?

CYNTHIA. I have wine and scotch.

BILL. Well, actually…

CYNTHIA. Oh, my god. Bill, I am so sorry.

BILL. Don't worry about it.

CYNTHIA. I totally forgot.

BILL. Please, Cynthia…

CYNTHIA. I can't believe how stupid I am.

BILL. Cynthia. Forget it. Really, it is not a big deal.

CYNTHIA. I have seltzer and lime.

BILL. That sounds great.

> (**CYNTHIA** *walks off stage left.* **BILL** *lifts up one of the diamonds and holds it up to the light.* **CYNTHIA** *returns with two glasses of seltzer with lime. She puts them down and sits across from* **BILL**. *She lifts her glass.*)

CYNTHIA. To posing.

BILL. I am not toasting until you get a proper drink.

CYNTHIA. This is fine.

BILL. Get a proper drink.

CYNTHIA. I don't need…

BILL. Get a proper drink.

CYNTHIA. Bill…

BILL. Get a proper drink.

(CYNTHIA lowers her glass, stares at BILL for a moment, and then walks off stage left. BILL holds the other diamond up to the light. CYNTHIA returns with a glass of white wine.)

Sure. Drink in front of a recovering alcoholic.

CYNTHIA. Don't joke. I feel bad.

BILL. *(He lifts his glass.)* To posing.

(BILL and CYNTHIA toast and then drink. They put their glasses down and look at each other.)

CYNTHIA. It really is nice to see you.

BILL. Yeah. It's been way too long.

CYNTHIA. Your e-mail was cute.

BILL. Really? I was afraid the hand-job reference might have crossed the line.

CYNTHIA. Oh please. When have your dirty jokes ever offended me?

BILL. People change. *(pause)* I've actually become more careful. You'd be surprised.

CYNTHIA. It was cute. *(pause)* How did you get my e-mail?

BILL. I bumped into Jen at an art gallery in L.A.

CYNTHIA. Oh, that's right. She told me about that.

BILL. She filled me in on all of your…developments.

CYNTHIA. Yes. There's been a lot of those.

(CYNTHIA goes to the glass case and picks up her eye piece and tweezers. She returns to her chair.)

OK. Shall we begin?

BILL. Please.

CYNTHIA. You mentioned in your e-mail that Linda wants something unconventional.

BILL. Laura.

CYNTHIA. I'm sorry. Laura.

BILL. Yes. Unconventional. I want to avoid cliché.

CYNTHIA. I think you mentioned a sapphire.

BILL. Emerald.

CYNTHIA. Right, an emerald. *(pause)* Well, as you can see, these are not emeralds.

BILL. Yes. I did notice that.

CYNTHIA. These are diamonds. They are very similar in shape and weight, only this one is slightly more flawed.

(**CYNTHIA** *picks up the diamond with her tweezers and observes it through an eye piece.*)

There are two tiny inclusions near the center of the stone. Here, have a look.

(**CYNTHIA** *gently hands him the diamond and the eye piece.* **BILL** *looks at it.*)

Do you see the inclusions?

BILL. I'm not sure.

CYNTHIA. Here. Look at this one.

(**CYNTHIA** *gives him the other diamond to look at.*)

BILL. Wow. Yes. This one is much more clear. There is so much light.

CYNTHIA. Isn't it beautiful?

BILL. It really is. Yes.

(**BILL** *puts the stone down and picks up his drink.*)

It sort of clarifies the word "bling" for me.

CYNTHIA. Exactly. That diamond will refract the light more brilliantly. It glitters.

BILL. It's dazzling.

(*There is a silence as* **BILL** *stares down at the diamonds.*)

CYNTHIA. Are you still thinking emerald.

BILL. No. No.

CYNTHIA. I mean, I can show you some very nice emeralds.

BILL. No. I like the diamond.

(**BILL** *continues staring down at the diamonds. There is a long silence.*)

CYNTHIA. Bill?

BILL. Yes?

CYNTHIA. Is everything alright?

BILL. Yes. *(pause)* Actually, no. I guess things are not alright.

CYNTHIA. Do you want to talk about it?

BILL. No. It's really nothing.

CYNTHIA. Ok.

BILL. Laura is really wonderful.

CYNTHIA. I'm sure she is.

BILL. Cynthia?

CYNTHIA. Yes?

BILL. I don't love her.

CYNTHIA. What?

BILL. I do not love this woman, Cynthia.

(*They look at each other.* **CYNTHIA** *picks up the diamonds and returns to her position behind the glass case.* **BILL** *picks up her glass of wine and takes a sip.*)

I do not love her. *(pause)* I don't think I ever loved her.

CYNTHIA. Bill.

BILL. I don't want to do this.

CYNTHIA. So, why are you doing it?

BILL. I don't know.

CYNTHIA. That is not true. You must know.

BILL. She needs me.

CYNTHIA. She needs you?

BILL. I *think* she needs me. I *believe* she needs me.

(**CYNTHIA** *goes to him. She pulls her chair beside him.*)

I'm sorry.

CYNTHIA. Don't be sorry.

BILL. I am. This is really not…

CYNTHIA. Bill. Do not feel bad.

BILL. I just wanted to see you.

> (**BILL** *touches her cheek gently with his hand. He holds his hand to her cheek for a moment.* **CYNTHIA** *gets up from her chair slowly and walks back to the showcase. She begins to put the diamonds away.*)

I just wanted to see you.

CYNTHIA. OK. You've seen me.

BILL. I'm sorry.

CYNTHIA. You already said that.

BILL. Don't be upset.

CYNTHIA. I'm not upset. I just need to close up now.

BILL. You can't say you didn't want to see me, Cynthia.

CYNTHIA. Of course I wanted to see you. *(pause)* But, you came here for an engagement ring.

> (**BILL** *gets up and walks behind the glass case. He stands in front of her.*)

BILL. Come have a drink with me.

CYNTHIA. What are you talking about?

BILL. I just want to have a drink.

CYNTHIA. No. I'm sorry.

BILL. You cannot tell me that this was just about selling me a diamond. You cannot tell me that.

CYNTHIA. It was not just about selling you a diamond. Of course, I wanted to see you.

BILL. It was more than that.

CYNTHIA. No.

BILL. You look so beautiful.

CYNTHIA. Do not do this.

BILL. Just have one drink with me. Please, Cynthia.

> (**BILL** *pulls her close to him and kisses her.*)

CYNTHIA. Do not do this.

> *(blackout)*

OTHER TITLES AVAILABLE FROM SAMUEL FRENCH

SUBCULTURE

Steve Yockey

Ten Minute Plays / Various m and f

Two men at the end of the world, a woman who believes she turns children to stone, some college students with alcohol and a sledgehammer, the perpetrator of a hit-and-run accident, a man obsessed with asphyxiation, and a roadside elephant in India. The very broken characters that inhabit this collection of shorts wander through a dimly lit, over stimulated and paranoia-fueled world that exists just underneath the dominant popular culture. From the darkly comic to the starkly distressing, these uneasy little plays are tightly wound, structurally adventurous glimpses into some of the most simultaneously intimate and harrowing moments of everyday life.

Contains:
(every little thing)
sucker punch
kiss & tell
dizziness & loss of breath
snuff film
lonesome
stop motion
swallow
(stereo) headphones
medusa

SAMUELFRENCH.COM

www.ingramcontent.com/pod-product-compliance
Lightning Source LLC
Chambersburg PA
CBHW070648300426
44111CB00013B/2323